Geography Lessons

Melissa Rendlen

Clare Songbirds Publishing House Poetry Series
ISBN 978-1-947653-90-0
Clare Songbirds Publishing House
Geography Lessons © 2020 Melissa Rendlen

All Rights Reserved. Permission to reprint individual poems must be obtained from the author who owns the copyright.

Printed in the United States of America
FIRST EDITION

Clare Songbirds Publishing House was established to provide a print forum for the creation of limited edition, fine art from poets and writers, both established and emerging. We strive to reignite and continue a tradition of quality, accessible literary arts to the national and international community of writers, and readers. Chapbook manuscripts are carefully chosen for their ability to propel the expansion of art and ideas in literary form. We provide an accessible way to promote the art of words in order to resonate with, and impact, readers not yet familiar with the siren song of poets and writers. Clare Songbirds Publishing House espouses a singular cultural development where poetry creates community and becomes commonplace in public places.

140 Cottage Street
Auburn, New York 13021
www.claresongbirdspub.com

Contents

Eagles Return to Oneida County	7
Into the Waves	8
Water Marks	9
Sitting in the Shade in the Valley of the Sun	10
Aftermath	11
The Park Bench	12
A Daughter Visits the Memory Unit	13
I Claim Today	14
Footprints	15
Dust	16
A Fisherman	17
Dearly Departed	18
Desert's Daughter	19
Last Blood	20
Thief	21
The Northwoods	22
A Cabin	23
Inner Walls	24
Resound	25
Within	26
Self Portrait With Oranges	27
ask nothing	28
Growing Up in the Desert in the Age of Water Coolers	29
Note to a Formal Garden	30
Fishing on Lake Enterprise	31
A Letter to My Brother	32
May Your New Year Be Good	33
Kayaking After the Storm	34
Sit Quietly	35

The author wishes to thank the following journals for the initial publication of these poems.

GFT Press: "A Note to a Formal Garden"
" Into the Waves"

Ink in Thirds: "A Cabin"

L'Ephemere: "Dust"
"The Northwoods"

The Light Ekphrastic: "Fishing on Lake Enterprise"

The Missing Slate: "Dearly Departed"

Nixes Mate: "Growing Up In the Desert In the Age of Water Coolers"

Plath Poetry Project: "ask nothing"
"Fishing On Lake Enterprise"
"Inner Walls"
"Resound"
"Sitting In the Shade In the Valley of the Sun"
"Thief"
"Water Marks"

Still Crazy: "Within"

Synkroniciti: "Eagles Return to Oneida County"

Underfoot Poetry: "Desert's Daughter"
"Kayaking After the Storm"
"Sit Quietly"
"The Park Bench"

Writing Raw: "Footprints"

For my daughters, Marietta and Elizabeth
If you consider me a good person, that is enough.

Eagles Return to Oneida County

*The first sighting of Bald Eagles in Oneida
county in more than twenty years was
reported May 18, 2016.*

I tell you I saw them, a pair, as they soared over the lake.
In my kayak I followed, watched them land at the top
of an ancient white pine at the center of the island.
Their one hundred foot tree showed its age,
bare branches bent in angles at the top,
perfect for eagles perch and eaglets nest.

For days, I paddled out to watch them watch the lake.
Their gaze unwavering, followed fish schools in the shallows,
found the loon's nest hidden within the reeds.

The wary loons ventured out, babies on their backs.
took turns diving into the depths, rejoined
their mate, fed the chicks riding on its back
before chicks ventured to swim nearby.

One eagle rose,
gathered his wings,
turned and dove,
snatched first one chick,
then the next,
returned to feed
the eaglets in his nest.

Into the Waves

Like our mothers thirty years before,
in Grandfather's wooden canoe,
we learned to paddle out into the waves.

Each bay, sand bar, and rock bed
mapped inside my head.

We paddled the shoreline, eased
through reeds, brushed over lily pads.

We heard the canoe's canvas cover
slip through deep green water,
soughing like the trees.

When our shadows outgrew us we turned
and let the wind push us home again.

Water Marks

Wondrous child,
small fingers that grasp
for my unobtainable hand.

Sun obscured
by clouds, the mother
of rain, muddy stains

across the nursery floor.
My bare footprints
circle,

trail out the door,
unmask
your sun and stars.

Sitting in the Shade in the Valley of the Sun

Above the pool white adobe walls
curve behind bougainvillea,
decorative palm, well planted cactus,
an oasis between red rock hills
covered in sajuaro and prickly pear.
Blue sky too wide,
unending sun seems inviting
as I sit at shaded poolside.

Soft comfort belies the desert's
harsh realities, where rattlesnake
and gila monster wait,
predators watching for prey.
Jumping cactus hurl pieces
of themselves
at unsuspecting hands
or feet that stray too close.

Desert heat escalates
between shadeless cactus.
We believe we have tamed
the untamable.
The ineradicable desert
toys with us,
smiles, waits.

Aftermath

Shredded relics, plastic bags
roll, roll, roll
down deserted streets,
snag on dying weeds,
congregate down alleyways.
Deep in recesses
men huddle, hoodies up,
backs to the wind.
They lean in,
cup scarred hands
as matches flicker,
light tattered cigarettes.

The Park Bench

Every day, a walk,
made ever more slowly
past once elegant
brownstones.
At the park they
ease onto their worn
wooden bench.
Stiff, they seem
to shrink as they settle.
Their faces in repose,
a silent stillness
surrounding, gives
an aura of waiting.
He in faded fedora,
torn topcoat,
she hidden, wrapped
within woolen scarf,
ancient mink, long
frayed at the shoulders.
A barely perceptible
movement, their fingers
searching for their mate's,
entwine, hold on.

A Daughter Visits the Memory Unit

Shapes try to form
                lost in the cobwebbed wood
        that is my mind.

I try to brush them away,
            they stick,
thick and thicker,
            entangled,
     too close to focus.

A face
      looks into mine,

                drifts.

                        Her eyes question.

A woman

                kneels before me,

takes my hands in hers,

so gentle.

                She kisses my forehead.

I Claim Today

Today is mine,
no matter whether
given or won.
Uncompromising
it walks erect,
strides towards night.

Robust in its aspirations
I will not relinquish it
to ghostly fears,
demons of inaction,
those thieves of moments.

Each minute mine!
Each thought and sorrow mine.

The heat of summer's day,
sun upon the lake,
snowfall in the street light,
belong to me.

Each fall, each scar,
belongs to me.

They will not be lost
in casualness or haste.
Come at me if you must,
the waste of time yours,
not mine.

Footprints

Deep within the woods
two lines of daffodils
form a path long
since overgrown.

As I walked the deserted
path the scent of a blooming
lilac announced itself. Bits
of foundation, rusted hand pump,
and leaning outhouse fixed in time
the long departed residents.

Far from neighbor and from town
what quiet, hard lives must have
been lived here.

And yet, in fall
one hundred years ago, I imagine

a woman in faded dress,
face older than her years,
with hands that had seen
too many wash days,

kneeling to plant two rows
of perfectly parallel,
yellow daffodils.

Dust

Laughter abandoned,
an animated face
turns slack.

Vacant stares replace
bright eyes, revealing
the brown, brittle

leaves that now reside
within your brain. Bone
drips into veins,

deserting as body bends,
breaks with such slight
weight. Melting

muscle, wasted flesh
on a skeleton too frail
for support.

The pull of the earth
reclaims the dust
that once was you.

A Fisherman

A breeze spread sunlight
across the lake.
In the center
of this brightness
a dark silhouette,
stark, stood
in his fishing boat.
For a moment the fisherman
air, sky, and I
brilliantly bathed
in reflected light.

Decades ago, my father and I
sat in a fishing boat
on this lake.

He set my line shorter.
You'll catch all the fish, he said.
I watched as he caught fish instead.

Today's azure sky
suddenly gone,
turned gunmetal grey.
A chill shadow
separated me from the light
as clouds moved
between earth and sun.
My gaze turned from sky to water.
The fisherman was gone.

Dearly Departed

                My Father's daughter is dead.

I know because I buried her.

                She lies at the bottom of a grave,
                curled on her side. A little girl
                in a little blue dress, red ringlets tied in ribbons.

I shoveled soft, dark dirt on top of her.
Shovel, by shovel, by shovel.
                First I covered her feet, clad in hated red shoes,
                then her ankles with white, perfectly folded socks.

Slowly, I worked my way up her legs,
over her belly to her chest.
                I covered her outstretched hands,
                her face, her open eyes, her shut mouth.

Bend, scoop, twist, toss.
Bend, scoop, twist, toss.

Shovel, after shovel, after shovel
                until a mound rose above the ground.

Then I knelt, planted one by one
                lilies, daffodils, roses, hollyhocks.

Desert's Daughter

In early spring desert air changes
from dust to green, the sun
not murderous, but soft,
makes ocotillos bloom.
In summer for a respite
from the heat we spent
weekends in Prescott.
Surrounded by ponderosa pine
we watched horses round the far
turn of the half mile track, cheering
them on with our nickel bets.
On our way home we'd stop
at a little cafe for homemade
tamales, rice, and beans.
Halfway down the mountain
burros inhabited the roadside
rest, dared rock strewn
cliff in hopes of carrots.

In March I watch the Midwest
snow, remember sitting atop
North Mountain, feel the breeze,
smell the rain, see storms
cross the Valley of the Sun.
Memory mixed with pain.
I cry for my desert home
and the broken, isolated
me, the fractured family
I had to flee, leaving you
behind. Distance
the only mend.

Last Blood

Words wrap around letters,
tight like Christmas packages.
A present with a surprise, tied
with a bow made by an evil elf,
delivered with malice and a smile.

Thrust and parry used to be more fun,
now cruel twists disguised as humor.
When love disintegrates
we forget how to be adults.

Anger more gratifying than reason
the person within a person,
a murderer released. Our Tarot,

Death of the Lovers. Blades
engage, letters become words
that become letters
we should not have sent.

Restraint not part of the rules.
Foils off, masks discarded we
advance, our dance of romance
foreplay to destruction.

First blood yours.
Last blood mine.

Thief

A stale moon sets in my window.

Its fluorescence flickers, a false light
plays peek-a-boo across your back
as you slither and slink
out of my yard.

You run under autumn trees,
through blowing leaves,
you play tag with the moon.
You hide, now gone.

Steal away.
Steal what was mine.

You run to the other side of town,
to the whore who never sees the moon
except from her backside.

The Northwoods

As I drive alone down the highway
soft air slips through open windows.

The woods, meadows,
sunlight after the rain
so like my woods
a lake and state away.
There, white papered birches
glow beside dark hemlocks,
form families under giant white pines.

In these unknown woods, just like home,
dark oiled log cabins with weathered
rock chimneys, sit down pine needle
covered driveways, dot lake shores.

These are not the cabins, logs,
or lakes that witnessed the first fish
I caught, or heard our teenaged chatter
as we walked along the road.

Only our maples, birch and white pines
stood vigil as we spent afternoons
laughing on piers, took turns learning to ski.
Only our cabin logs watched rainy day
jigsaw puzzles, evening games of Hearts
and Spades, saw us grow up and go away.

Now we drive on unknown roads
through unfamiliar woods.

A Cabin,

just logs
facing a lake.
Summers spent
in woods and on water.
This drowning child's
life raft.

Inner Walls

Hollow night.
Blackness hovers outside
the ring of light.
No drop of shoe
or slam of door resonates.
In a car's lights rain
turns to ice.
Despair trapped
in an oversized chair,
upholstery worn thin
where hands reside.
Feet still against the floor
as revolutions inside my head
paralyze.
Intention a lost concept.

Resound

You, who speak of words,
their unending echoes,

a sonic blast—
silenced.

Irreversible acts resound.

A riderless horse
wanders afield, left

to eat through bitted mouth,
looks for a path home.

You, Houdini under ice
no seance can raise.

Your words, razor's edge,
drip red across the page.

The only mother we will ever know.

Within

I am the loon
diving down into cool
waters, more at home
in these depths
than in air.
Flying through murky water
I snatch my prey, then dart
above the waves again.
On summer afternoons
you will see me floating,
babies on my back.
When I take flight
I am a low flying missile
the beating of my wings shouts
Incoming!
My nightly cry comes
from the center of the earth,
primordial.

Self Portrait With Oranges

        i
her first twenty Aprils
filled with acres
of orange blossoms

        ii
she walked alleys
picked oranges that hung
over neighbors' fences
unseen he watched

        iii
his thumb pushed against
the knobby flesh
his nail ripped the skin
inner fruit exposed
dripped over his hand

        iv
cement and condominiums
replaced desert and citrus groves
reflect inescapable heat

        v
she no longer remembers
warm April nights the scent
of orange blossoms on the air

        vi
a man waits
an orange blossom
in his lapel

        vii
snow falls like petals
silences her landscape
ripe oranges rot at her feet

        viii
she walks empty handed
bears no fruit
leaves no footprints

ask nothing

fool's expectations
hope's plaything

scattered over
hot sands

evaporates

with the desert
dew   leaves

body prostrate

sun bores
blinds eyes

bleaches bone

immovable limbs
numb mind

ask nothing

Growing Up in the Desert in the Age of Water Coolers

Once a summer the evening news
fried an egg on a car hood.
Humidity crept up,
made water coolers useless,
turned homes to saunas.

Two weeks in August,
a trip to the Pacific,
a motel near the beach.
Our car un-airconditioned,
we were put to bed at eight,
maybe asleep at midnight,
awakened at three, a pre dawn
trek across the desert.
My brother and I bundled
in the back seat,
slept.

Our old Pontiac crept
through the dark desert,
the sky filled with milky way.
We made our way up mountain passes
strewn with boulders,
then down to the Colorado.
We reached Needles at dawn
in time for gas and breakfast,
sleep forgotten, replaced
with anticipation.

By eleven
the smell of the ocean,
then a beautiful sunlit blue
sparkled to the horizon.
Over days I became
the salt, the water,
the crash of waves.

Note to a Formal Garden

The world before gardens,
your ancestor, whispers to you.
Primeval roots give birth to branches,

branches reach, grow leaves,
blow in the ancient wind.

They beckon you from paved path,
manicured yard, well kept hedgerow.

Return to your birthplace,
to the natural child that grew inside you.

Return to every child turned man before you.

Become a part of unkempt hedge,
wild meadow, untamed wind—

Shine.

Fishing On Lake Enterprise

In June cabins around lakes
fill with generations. Parents
become grandparents,
children become parents.
Old couples relinquish
ski tows, dot the lake
in fishing boats. Afternoons
on piers intertwine families,
form chains that circle the shore.

From my dock I watch
my neighbors'
slow procession
down steep steps,
before rattle of footfall
along their pier.
Lew in wrinkled flannel
over paint stained T,
cigarette hanging from
his mouth, helps Betty laden
with thermos of martinis,
hamper of sandwiches.
They settle among fishing nets,
and poles, begin the slow crawl
toward rock bed, weeded bay.

Their outings lengthen
through shortening days.
We close our cabin, make
rounds of *See you next summer's!*
Our last stop saved
for Betty and Lew.
She helps him into their boat,
says they'll stay through fall.

The next year we return.
Their boat has been sold.
Betty says it was too hard
to start the pull cord motor alone.

A Letter to My Brother

Sandpipers chase tides,
run along water's edge.
The sound of sea gulls,
shouts of children unchanged
from summers long ago.
How hot the sand was
as we dragged beach towels
the wide expanse from parking
lot to waters' edge. A quick drop
of flip flops, towels and snacks
before we threw ourselves
into the Pacific. Day after day
sand between our toes,
lodged in swimsuits,
as salt water dried upon our skin.

Each year we ventured further out,
then to the final breakers so we
could catch the largest waves.
Remember when we swam beyond
the furthest swell, caught the largest wave?
We rode it halfway back before it tumbled us
in somersaults, pounded us against
the ocean floor. I held my breath

until I had none. My chest burned and split
as hands and eyes sought light, we wild,
helpless to the water's whim until the wave,
spent, tossed us back on shore.

May the New Year Be Good

May the year to come be good to you and those you love.

May the tormented find peace,
the homeless refuge,
the greedy become generous.

May care replace neglect,
unity replace division,
love replace hate.

May leaders be wise.

May we see that with each simple act we change the world.

May our acts be kind.

Kayaking After the Storm

Wind picks up, rain drops,
then a curtain of rain pounds,
crosses from opposite shore.
A fishing boat's drone heard
as it heads for home.
The drum of rain constant
on the cabin roof, inhabitants
settle in, wait with books
or jigsaw puzzles, watch
for the storm to end.

Dark clouds move east, sun
appears in the west. Calm
water stretches shore to shore,
the echo of a dog's bark, slam
of cabin doors announce
the storm over as birds chirp
and ruffle. I move to lake
edge, climb in rain soaked
kayak, head west through
waveless water. Blue sky
grows as clouds leave,
sun lowers. I reach the western shore,
turn home. A barely perceptible breeze
pushes. I rest my paddle, float.

Ahead of me a dark shape
transforms to loon. A slow,
quiet approach,
I keep my paddle still.
He preens after the storm.
Gradually closer,
I expect him to dive.
He cleans first one wing,
then the other, then back.
Not twenty feet away
he lifts his belly into the air,
each feather visible,
black bill works intently.
Waves carry me past.

Sit Quietly
you my/ bright particular
Letter Poem #3 James Schulyer

After supper, sit quietly.
                    Watch the fleeting fireflies as dusk becomes dark.

Attend the constellations within our planet.

A timpani of bullfrogs resonates
                    under stars that shimmer, heavens that expand.

The smell of jasmine and mown grass in summer air
                    caresses cheek, fondles shoulder,

surrounds,
                    enfolds us in that bright particular.

Melissa Rendlen has been a practicing ER/Urgent care physician for thirty-eight years, although she is now enjoying pseudo-retirement. She has finally moved to her beloved Northwoods of Wisconsin where she loves to hike, kayak, and just hang out. Many of her poems are centered around observations from this area. She has had poetry published in *The Missing Slate, Nixes Mate Review* and anthology, *Voice* anthology, *Poets Reading the News, Indolent Press What Rough Beast, Underfoot Poetry, L'ephemera, The Light Ekphrastic*, and *Synkroniciti*. This is her first chapbook.

www.ingramcontent.com/pod-product-compliance
Lightning Source LLC
Chambersburg PA
CBHW052129110526
44592CB00013B/1811